Sheepshead Bay

Also by Ed Barrett

Common Preludes

Sheepshead Bay

Ed Barrett

WITHDRAWN

𝒵
ZOLAND BOOKS
Cambridge, Massachusetts

First edition published in 2001 by
Zoland Books, Inc.
384 Huron Avenue
Cambridge, Massachusetts 02138

Copyright © 2001 by Edward Barrett

All rights reserved. No part of this book may be used or reproduced
in any manner whatsoever without written permission, except in the
case of brief quotations embodied in critical articles or reviews.

FIRST EDITION

Book design by Boskydell Studio

Printed in the United States of America

05 04 03 02 01   8 7 6 5 4 3 2 1

This book is printed on acid-free paper, and its binding
materials have been chosen for strength and durability.

Library of Congress Cataloging-in-Publication Data
Barrett, Edward.
Sheepshead Bay / Ed Barrett.
p. cm.
ISBN 1-58195-103-5
I. Title
PS3552.A7339 S48 2001
811'.54—dc21   2001026132

Cover photograph: Sheepshead Bay, 1967,
courtesy of the author.

PS
3552
.A7339
S48
2001

DEC 0 6 2001

For Jennie

Acknowledgments

The author gratefully acknowledges the following publications in which versions of poems in *Sheepshead Bay* first appeared: *can we have our ball back? Brooklyn Review, Key Satch(el), lift, Lingo, Meanie, My Friends, The Newark Review, Pressed Wafer, Talisman.*

The poems "By No Stretch of the Imagination," "Jigs and Reels," "Practical Lullabies for Joe," "The Same Sad Song They Whistle in the Future," "Peripheral Vision," "For the Moment," and "The American Opera" first appeared in *Watteau Sky*, a chapbook collaboration with Joe Torra, published by Quale Press with artwork by Gian Lombardo.

"Letter in Latin to Bill in Vermont" originally appeared in *The Blind See Only This World*, a collection of broadsides for John Wieners, published by Granary Books/Pressed Wafer.

The author is grateful to the Massachusetts Cultural Council for a generous grant which helped support the writing of this book.

Contents

THE SONNETEER

    The Sonneteer 3
    Goethe Did Not Invent Physics To
       Murder Anyone 4
    Sinn Fein Gorli Drogue 5
    The Lighthouse Family 6
    O Jerusalem 7
    Tír na nÓg 8

PRACTICAL LULLABIES FOR JOE

    By No Stretch of the Imagination 11
    Jigs and Reels 13
    Practical Lullabies for Joe 15
    The Same Sad Song They Whistle
       in the Future 17
    Peripheral Vision 18
    For the Moment 20
    The American Opera 21

THE IRONBOUND

    The Ironbound 25
    Lost Science 26
    Traffic Island 27
    Billie Burke in Grand Central Station 28

ACCUSATIVE OF PLACE

    Letter in Latin to Bill in Vermont 31
    Naming Race Horses 34
    Pilgrims Undaunted by Speed 38

Summer Baby 39
A Vision of Ted Berrigan in Cambridge,
   Massachusetts 42
All the While Knowing 44
How People Swim 46
The Mummy 48
Boston Italy 49

CIGARETTE, GIOTTO, TOUGH GUY

Kerry Set for Joe Brainard 53
   French Blue Jacket
   Lycidas Algorithm
   The Living End
   Flame Coat
Intimations of Immortality 64
Archery 67
Three Italian Sonnets for Mark Morris 69
Night for Day 71

LYRICAL BALLADS

Lyrical Ballads 75
Antigone in Flatbush 76
Two Poems for Kenward Elmslie 81
   Snow
   Untitled
Secent Image 84
Song 88

The Sonneteer

What did I tell you? Look at the chin. He's a killer all right.

The Petrified Forest

The Sonneteer

I have surveilled this region day and night and still no trace of you. I must have been crazy buying reconnaissance software called *The Sonneteer* ("Because Life Is A Lesson In Grammar, A Series Of Endings!" "Direct Matters With Surprising Affection, Almost A Kind Of Knowledge About Life and Death, Dreaded As Thou Art!"). It offered to reach into the cone-shaped throat of darkness with my voice as through the surface of an icy stream, like a child trying to get at a shiny stone. Even the stars were warm and trashy; memory, my portion of recognition fated to be in there ("If Something Turns Into Something Else, Wasn't It Always That?"), inevitable and just as the Harry Warren tune *You'll Never Know* in which love parted its lips and sang *if you don't know now*.

Goethe Did Not Invent Physics to Murder Anyone
for Pierre Martory

Goethe did not invent physics to murder anyone, and my memory crosses near him to place a very pretty plum-colored scarf around your neck as if it were a cravat, or even just the notion that we would say cravat. Goethe emerges in his *Theory of Colors* in German with the curve of the mountain road paring the apple of distance or emulation or sex (the scarf, let me remind you) of its skin until, just a little bit farther on, it twists into the sweetest little parish. Did you ever see such a pretty place? And just look who's coming out to say hello! In the scarf a purely German physical tumult, soft as the figures on the skin of a plum, the ghostly part is on fire. Hello, they say, hel-lo, why, we'd thought you'd never get here, just look at you! and hug you so tight because physics can't tell you everything before they cross over into memory. And these platelets of color — the scarf, the road, skin — speak to Goethe as if he were a plum! Imagine that, Goethe, the great German poet who needs no introduction, a plum. His violet theory of tumult says you have these things as something else, which is your usual theory approach, platelets of color rushing toward the open wound of the day to staunch it from bleeding too far into that something else. Commando-action Goethe, Wolfgang the Goth, Wolfman, "old wild Wolf" sees it crossing his vacant shadow like an early school bell in camouflage pants. And is he scared? Hello, they say, hello-ee-lo-lo.

Sinn Fein Gorli Drogue

for John Ashbery

My children, said the wall and fell silent . . . "again" or "forever," intervals arguing their separate spastic musical theorems like gangplanks or Dutch beds, arguments plump as the side of a hay barn about to burst into flame, "my children" attaching less of everything to something, some one thing that cannot be resolved, not even "for" example, and therefore true and out of reach. Surely everything gets banked up against something somewhere, like these immortal plastic shopping bags stuck in the trees, something which saves it from drifting away until you don't notice it anymore, so that the cabinet doors rattle like crazy until a bed pops out fully made, pillows fat as ravioli bouncing a couple of times on top of the covers because of their absolute perfection. Makes you want to bounce on the covers too. In your drawers. My children said the wall as if it were going deeper inside itself like a musical theorem in Boston, which appears self-evident once you see it written out, death somehow mysteriously already drifting through you. The plump Dutch silence of the sky carrying two big buckets of milk from the barn cannot get into this style of argument unless it has a bouncy rhythm to set its clogs tapping like a mechanical knitting machine. Click click click go the needles, tapping blindly down the itchy path they weave. My children said the wall as if these stones, this music could speak, not about some secrets of their nature, but to us, as if we were theirs to love, and they did love us for ourselves alone.

The Lighthouse Family

for William and Beverly Corbett

child of earth
— WILLIAM WORDSWORTH

It's enough to know what's coming and then not to live within the gauge with a thin coppery smile. A new jacket, for example, transforms "alot" into mechanical movements, salmony equations of expectation and independence, independence derived from expectations, not as you might want to christen them causes, not even results with bits of straw stuck in their hair, but a taste for some things which serves as a reminder that you are not just pulled along in the tide, so that this thought breaks through one of the Seven Seas in a lonely way sometimes, or maybe you feel like someone hacked into your memory and downloaded secret tapes of conversations that sound marvelously prophetic, life-like dreams remastered with you spending a night with the lighthouse family, salvers gleaming with fruits of sea-wrack and ruin, woe, and later, singing and drinking and looking for shooting stars. Is it not possible, asks the engineering genius, that someday the path may be established more directly? But the world as meditation ravels and unravels its sailors in black watch caps and bell bottoms, moves rubies around from jeweler to skin condition in a very prodigal manner. Who are you to think like a beacon piercing the ocean of night like that? And what do you get out of it? It must've been something I lost, is the reply you may use, just something I lost, OK? And no one will mention it again. And it will be transmitted to generations of evenings, buff-colored as a baseball, streaked with green light and grass stains, a piece of film with sprockets along the edge where the teeth bite in, dusted light from the projection room widening like a boat's wake in the air above the movie theater where we drown and laugh.

O Jerusalem

for Trevor Winkfield

Not a true Palatinate red, Caravaggio steals the body of Christ from connection with the Dublin airport, a design point for the really naked, the really helpless, who don't collect around things like this. What would you propose to do about it? Your own soul, for example, wandering in the lime-green light of the night-vision goggles the Army uses? The body of truth collapses through the arms of the helpless, a swale of nakedness where spring flowers such as Stinking Benjamin shy their little panties at your head when you take a peep: they're pollinated by turban-eyed flies, which causes the stink, as opposed to bees, which are cleaner. Caravaggio steals the lime-green body of Christ, his hand tipped slowly into evening, betraying the novelistic whole with a kiss. Why would he vouchsafe such pash-ee-o-net things to us? How will our nakedness show it, our soul which is about the size of a linnet? The body dies and the soul most likely dies with it although each rendezvous seemed out of time, all chocolatey and nice, yet embroidered somehow into the puffy velvet sleeve of its embrace.

Tír na nÓg

Virgil held a blood-filled syringe and sang in perfect epic feet, *You'll never know if you don't know now,* and his words fell short of the kind of beautiful grouting work he is justly famous for, but they had an idle, menacing beauty. And I remember the fear I felt, small and leafy, as once when I was a boy I rowed at low tide into the mouth of a storm drain at the end of Sheepshead Bay careful not to scrape against the walls and roof. The Virgin Mary held the mouth of the storm drain open for a minute while I let myself out. It was a close call because when you do things like that, the laws of nature can be repealed and the tide turn suddenly — although this has never, ever happened in Brooklyn — and rush in, hurling me at my death from grandeur into one more thing floating in a world of shit. I believe this is what the syringe meant: it held my heart in its little glass-walled chamber, and you can imagine how I elected to jab it quickly into my arm.

Practical Lullabies
for Joe

By No Stretch of the Imagination

This poem is coming on the right day because I have stopped writing in the sense when someone sees me on Mass. Ave. and asks, "What are you writing?" or "Are you writing anything?" they mean what are you writing connected to or, pardon the word, programmatic of a longer thought or interval of experience which is filtered through poetic gills opening and closing on the side of the writer's face? This is why a poet may not be all that good looking although within the species these gill-organs of inspiration are hardly noticed, or perhaps noticed as a really attractive feature, like those brightly colored fig-like things on some monkey bottoms. "The body of thought" is a good phrase when it is reported that right after Deng Xiaoping's death his corpse was dissected and his corneas removed, two shimmering snails popped out of their shells, so that a comrade may no longer tread this earth's salty crust in darkness, feeling with his or her feet the passage of events
so many people!   as cadence only. Now Comrade Deng-Eyes sees what before had been rumor: "like the rest of us" he thinks happily, for the first time in his life trying out this phrase as he once imagined using it, and straps to his feet the barrel staves of his former singular existence to ski away down the side of Mt. Life — in our mythology, with Jill St. John at his side. Their civilization, however, is too ancient not to have recognized they were really haruspicating around in his entrails, or to put it another way, while strip-mining his natural body, they were also looking for a saga of fate or destiny, which is what that question "What are you writing?" has become: what are you discovering "for the rest of us" to use as lenses to see into or through, or maybe for the first time, at? But where the troll bridge crossing says, Hmm, this will be meaningful, the road sometimes throws its face to the ground and cries; or

if I strike my forehead against the bronze-sandaled foot of the day, it is justice and love and knowledge I desire. But to be perfectly honest, I am lonely for Sheepshead Bay and my father and the boat we had. You should feel free to fill in the blanks about that statement as, metaphorically speaking, I walk around this room dressed like a gypsy violinist at Cafe Zwyzwyski, stopping at your table to whisper these lines while you talk or drink, allowing their music to become part of you, but I'm pretty certain about this: I have a very direct wish to feel on a daily basis sea spray coming over the bow and stinging my eyes, especially during the winter, and to wear bright yellow rubber pants held up by huge suspenders. A blind person's wish to see is no less real than this scene in my mind, and I feel I cannot see again without it, but where will I find the eyes to sew into my face to bring me to this boat? And how, if I don't, will I ever stop despising poetry?

Jigs and Reels

1.
In a funny way the present is just a vanishing point which you can see through like a screen which also supports your own reflection although you may not even have been cured. Because what do I see now that I am thinking of you and you had other sons who are looking at something else? Maybe one does not need to be cured at this moment. But you cannot hold that in reserve for when you do need a cure and therefore become a screen yourself, astonished that the cause of all that gazing into the washbasin could never be connected to the blossoming freshness of the extent of things as the portion of each refrain begins *as if anew* next to the rhetorical question *Maybe your other sons are dead and therefore it falls to me to argue this case from the bits of images ringing your name like a collar of ice.*

2.
If one looks in a mirror it is one's likeness reflected there. That is a rhetorical question which will not help if you say *I am blind* and therefore ignorant of the laws of fate and attraction because the outcome uses necessity. No one just as easily says *Look at this keyboard, it's impossible to make sense out of that, these must be lies!* and throws all the problems of language into the fire because the answer did not lie flat across the face of our natural expectation and desires, *natural* meaning anything I suppose, but not dismissive or the sense that there is no measure against which the projection of those expectations and desires should be judged. That would be crazy. Nevertheless we could see through even that, and it would add to this feeling of clarity, like ice-skating at night and the starry crystal hissing beneath your blades as they carve out dreams of what is after all voluble.

3.
For why would I be standing here like this, pleading a case for sufficiency only, in which affliction and the placement of effects carry you away to the end of something like a brook mindlessly fidgeting with its bra strap, although the terms of this argument are never very clear and decline recognition, in the grammatical sense, so that they become the immediate language of knowledge and memory, not in any passive way, not really *because of* but *by* them, how the outcome uses necessity as you float backwards through them to the truth?

4.
Immune to all this stuff, serious, not a matter for too much judgment, all intention and pleasure at the half door! Ultimately, you pick up on prodigality, thick as the mantle of fallen leaves: *What was I thinking?* raising your hand with the palm turned inward to give yourself a conk on the head; or: *these are sticks for my blindness,* one touch of a finger as the database swivels its hooded face to look at you, to look right through you, because the outcome uses necessity and the system is never overloaded or the reservoir drained to dangerously low levels because everyone knows it always fills up again.

Practical Lullabies for Joe

> this jade jar contains life
> — JOE TORRA

The curve of vision fails and wooden lines nailed to the floor

Your heart is a big lump of raw red meat. At night zombies come to eat it, but they are scared away by heart-eating cranes, which also fly in to feast.

Number the things you want in order of importance starting from your age now, and an example of knowing it's true.

I think you will discover there is no cure for the zombies/crane thing I mentioned earlier. The good news is it is rarely fatal; the bad news is the mess in the morning.

Baron Roger Von Crotchstein is a royal pain in the neck sometimes, isn't he?

For future reference: jade, the object and the word, I have never liked. The color jade is an absence of color. I pray I will never meet someone named Jade, especially if she pronounces it zsa-day.

Go to sleep, knowing the aggrieved have already chartered school-bus companies from now till the end of time, a yellow and black ribbon of certainty that stretches from the slopes of Areopagitica to America Online. Sleep, knowing they will not leave without you.

Dr. Hermann Von Languagestein is as difficult as his cousin the Baron.

Princess Zsa-Day then banished me from the kingdom, saying "That is an extremely valuable tale of connection, but they have no joy in knowing anything." For years, I planned insurrection: training with the US Navy Seals in Quantico, VA; then, for five years, living with a family of real seals off the Oregon coast. Seals by the way are huge pornographers: pictures of mollusks with their shells open — wide open — that sort of thing. They also are staunch believers in the First Amendment — *their* First Amendment which reads, "Death to all mollusks."

Never did I return to the kingdom of my banishment. Instead, I have chosen to live off the Oregon Coast among the pornographic but otherwise noble and kind seals. I don't give a crap about mollusks anyway. And tomorrow I receive the seals' highest honor: the Coral Wreath. Too bad I dislike coral as much as jade. I suppose I can live with it for where on this dustproof ocean will I go next? Who will take me in? And fate is endless.

The Same Sad Song They Whistle
in the Future

Devotional, and at sixty miles per hour
progressing, like an awful lot of bottles
near your head. Love
and an outdoor movie in daytime
would be different depending on how powerful
the projector is: either you could only
hear the sound without a picture,
a funny kind of unrelated story booming out,
surrounding the bushes,
or you could see grayish clay or
pastel erasures taking the form ideas have
before we speak them: random little errors
changing hands, your hair like nightfall,
columnar night marbled with smoke
rising out of our mouths, straying up past the inscription
above the capital: *In the Past, True*.
And in the present?
Paper hands night blows on to columns
and love casting erasures.

Peripheral Vision

wet book
— ANGE MLINKO

1.
Laughter, saw-toothed light, and through it all the edges of things unseen at first, turning out to be ample in themselves, complete, and in a sense not to be trusted, as when you look at anything up close it is jeweled beyond belief. The seasons therefore are another direction we have taken, a larger one and diagonal, going on above us like immense swatches of cloth to a patched and muddy field. You say it doesn't take much time. But the distance is not ours, the shout at the back of things which is falling away at such incredible speeds you hear it only as a sigh, tracing it in the path of these too-deliberate clouds shading across a river, plane over plane, enormous sheets of water. But during the day it is ropes.

2.
"Then what gets canceled now?" Something sailing marvelously, a single white ephemeron whose intemperate dance at this exquisite moment only signals that here is another bizarre expression we have failed to call to mind; that perspective does not exist, least of all the kind we want moving these dots around at night. Sounds are heard, or not. Distance exists, but only as the tightest bridge of single white ephemera. So it will not matter what the fates have done, disgusting things trying to rub themselves up against you. Out of these elements there is crystal: steep, goat-like steps slogging upward across selected streets. It is midtown in its most gigantic phase, and you its sweetest thief.

3.
These fragments, then, are like ice on that earliest morning when your breath comes in anticipation of something (you don't know what), but the air is so charged with connection, the sky so blue in its low curving, and the roads impassable. The day is studded with these, and your eyes are more like motes in sunlight than anything which is passing from layer to gemmed layer. There is no discourse we can hold with gorgeousness. Visions lose themselves along these spiny prisms, or we just get tired, the sails flump down around us still lashed ridiculously to the post. But we can return, and it will not be different, only less kind. Things will uncoil towards us, original colors will revive, plinth and lintel purl.

4.
I knew it was going to work that way, and could have said so "in that look" and meant it, too. "We all have secret palaces," you said, "I used to crawl down through the moss and pearls, where the French word for little whirlpool was. The stream was so cold it made me dizzy." Like so many of the things I know, I've heard the part about the true beginnings and the connections later on, the part about starry-pointed appearances in the shade, and I know this is what we mean by choice: more is hidden so we will want that too. Whatever happens could have happened. The important lessons are our own, welling up around us in the lawnchairs, and like the tide within the lawnchairs, so that we are surprised to find out where they turn up next. I say I know, but if it hadn't worked out that way, if on the other side I hadn't seen the silver line along the trees streaming into your hip, I wouldn't have known anything, all of it falling in behind me like a gulf.

For The Moment

> What is Watteau sky I imagine
> children . . . hunchbacked labor
> — JOE TORRA

It isn't innocent.
We live in cities because the countryside
isn't about to leap up around you in assistance
without cascading away again. Draw
the curtains, I mean, literally, draw them;
light the center. Then, like falling through
the texture of these things at their
stage of growth, a canopy over the bare
spot on the ground we find ourselves contained
in for the moment, about now, when the character
is ill-informed about the nature of the struggle
each one must endure, or that there has to be

a struggle, starting now, and later, all along,
at which time we learn how the contrast lingers,
the clarity absorbs the character of that first, trivial,
immense relationship of facts and figures,
how in each were honor and misfortune.
And the face hidden throughout: it was
your own likeness in the hills that day,
a lingering clarity the contrasts absorb,
how the story had sought no one.

The American Opera

This time the chef, who is really angry, bites the stub of his cigar so hard part of it splits off and falls into the empty frying pan he is holding in his right hand as he snarls at the pancake stuck to the ceiling. The American opera sweeps up the side of a moving bus to scrawl something, then heads for the rooftop pigeon coop, gently pulling the bottom part of some curtains outside a window. Mrs. Cacciatore leaves them there because it's hot out — besides, it's a way of accepting what's happening below is not a thought she is aware of having; it is a thought it is having about her, including her in the motions of the scene stirring into morning. From the rooftop, golden light makes buildings look like sheaves of wheat, but the pigeons know better and make one last swooping letter above the coop where they descend. The century appears to be ending as either a milkman or alien from another planet walks up the stoop and leaves something in a bottle by the door. Mr. Reginald van Hooten in top hat and tails, lurching home after last night's soiree, slurs "Hi everybody, my name's Charlie," apparently the punch line to his favorite joke. Instinct tells him nothing, and the liquor in his brain makes him forget where he lives so he never makes it upstairs where a thug is waiting to rob him. As the pancake falls from the ceiling, the figure of Death appears, finger crook'd on the first line of vellum, all flourishes in a royal hand — and doing what he does best, kills everyone except we discover it was merely a shadow of the real scene which he took away in his sack, a shadow created by the until this time apparently mad scientist who lived in the cellar under Mrs. Cacciatore. It was — no! — could it be? — yes! — Reginald van Hooten of the Advanced Institute who had perfected his duplicator ray. He was only covering his tracks, throwing off foreign spies by pretending to be a gadabout. All along she knew her faith in him wasn't misplaced, the lovely mayor's daughter before whose door he now stands, not with his usual supercilious smirk, but the true eyes of love as the street scene swells with citizens at a block party who never once doubt the stuff they're made of.

The Ironbound

The Ironbound

Really, if you want to make something out of it. And one grows restless at the thought. Or something precipitates out of the background noise with the kind of clarity I want in messages from life on other planets, or God: *my last name means blackberry* said someone I didn't really know yet, shyly, over the phone. This was an invitation to speak in Newark where I had taught for several years at an engineering school, first generation college students, sons (mostly) of New Jersey contractors who wanted to get out of the family business and work for the Environmental Agency or PSE&G, our version of Ovid's *Metamorphoses*. I think my entire lecture was an echo of that word blackberry, the simple act of translating one name into another name, with the slight conspiratorial feel it must have had for someone who teaches English as a Second Language: Did you know this? No? Well, what else might things mean? Or over lunch in a Portuguese restaurant in the Ironbound after my talk, feeling protected by the local politicians lunching with their mistresses, a strangely decorous display of, let's face it, how someone uses someone else, laced with the way one can fall in love too. It isn't always so easy. My host trusted me when he heard me order a martini, so he said that the day before he and his partner had registered at City Hall under the new law. This was followed by a toast and smiles and questions about what they wore and where they went afterwards, which is how we try to hold on to it, maybe how it tries to hold on to us too, reaching its hand over our hand, its shade-filled sleeve gaping like the mouth of cornucopia.

Lost Science

Life keeps its own in ways I don't understand yet. Each of us is a lost science. Things don't fit that well or get done with "surgical precision." There's too much wrong in the way we go about life for there to be nothing to spare. Too much wrong is part of the sequence, like narrative between arias, pushing the story along although I don't think the story ever needs to be pushed along and builds up enough steam of its own to pull us out of our cars and homes into the knotted middle of the river. You could put two people on a stage with a couple of props (memories of what we do when we don't think we're doing anything), then have the orchestra strike up, and a story would emerge naturally, or not "emerge" but they could tap into the story that is always curling just below the surface, scooping up mouthfuls of speech from that well. A lot of life is impersonal like this: not "ours" or at least not anyone's in particular until we make it ours, swim along in it for a while, or as when I was a boy on 14th Street we'd open a firepump and run through the spray when someone cupped their hands over the hydrant's mouth. That was an aria too, a boy's aria, not to be repeated by the same child later on, but certainly by someone else's child.

Traffic Island

There's plenty to spare, wanting to keep other things out of harm's way. Or some sign that it counted and that here was something or someone worth keeping because they were funny or kind or — the real cause — you loved them very much and they meant everything to you. The concrete pineapple over Atwell's Avenue like a deserted stage set and us climbing over chunks of plowed snow to the Thai restaurant. The Australian girl asking me (me!) for directions in Barcelona and her flower print dress, and how because it was hot, facing me, she turned her right leg out and rested her foot on a step and fanned herself with her skirt. Or putting a finger up to my lips so my mother wouldn't say anything as my father came in, and he turned and clapped his hands together like he was applauding something he must have wanted, and there I was, sitting at his table. The guy who sleeps by the river buying a six-pack of Bud at 10 AM gave a cause that did not explain but which domesticated the fissioning I was seeing, the instability I felt I stood on a rock above the other night because the mob owned the restaurant (so I'm told) and we could park on the white-striped traffic island, maybe a flashback to the only gift the father of a friend of mine could give me when he heard I was going away to a "good" school because he loved me and must have wanted to make me think he *could* send someone up there if anyone ever gave me any trouble, a dark thing to want to give your love to someone if you are a man. At least that's what I thought in my condition outside the restaurant, not knowing just what I was giving my love to, certainly not the mob and the night with blood on its hands, or those waiting inside who already had it, surely something I would understand when I saw it.

Billie Burke in Grand Central Station

for Bill Blake

Billie Burke? he used to ask when he told me this story, *Why would they be paging someone to meet the actress Billie Burke at Grand Central Station?* Why do you think when the name of what you really want is called, it sounds like something else? Why do you think when you go to the place where you will meet it, you don't recognize it? When he died, did his soul hover above his body listening for a name? *Then I knew* he used to smile as he pointed, *It was you,* the boy he was going to adopt dressed in a cowboy suit and, just to be sure, a bow and arrow slung over his shoulder.

◆

So maybe it is calling all the time. Maybe there is a good reason we can't hear it. I can't think of a good reason we can't hear it. I don't think we want anything else. I think we are talking about it when we are doing other things. I think it's crazy that we can't know it.

Accusative of Place

Letter in Latin to Bill in Vermont

for John Wieners

1.
I wonder what happened to Erika Schlumbermacher-Constantinebennettandsalami, too. When I was a kid I wanted to build a bathysphere covered with huge headlights like a thousand eyes and one big porthole for me to look at the bottom of Sheepshead Bay as I sailed silently and safely under the water. Once in a race with a friend to see who could swim farthest underwater, I flipped over on my back to do a frog kick, but with only the faint mimeograph-blue surface of the bay above me as my horizon I didn't realize I was going deeper until my head hit a crate covered with barnacles and seaweed. I said "ow," which if a startled fish nearby could hear, would have sounded like "ow-p-l." After that I was afraid to swim to the bottom because the barnacled crate, as I imagined it, surely contained severed body parts from a grisly murder. So a bathysphere, especially with headlights, would solve the problem of letting me swim underwater without having to fight off the murdered zombie people who lived in the waters around Brooklyn at that time.

2.
"Well, as you wrote, history only happens to us later on," and I was thinking I might like to have a bathysphere to swim back into some part of my life, but not as when one brushes coal dust off one's walrus mustache, sticks out one's chest, and in a throaty Irish brogue sings mining-company anthems as you stride out of the shaft with this or that chunk of bituminous spiritual ore of experience. MIT science says we are language and information and *communication*. But if I tell you that at the time of my childhood-bathysphere project, Lillian wore faded blue jeans so tight that the rough denim outlined her perfect

mound, and Jackie said, Will you look at that, and reached over and pinched it while she was standing there talking to Kathy, will the grammar of things rain softly through us: curved windows that looked out saltily to the bay; Jackie sliding backwards on his left foot after Lillian slapped him; gravel scattering away as he fell; and the sound of gravel as when you step onto it from a sidewalk like a sentence coming to its period after a few more inconsequential words?

3.
But neither do you want to spend a year writing *Ecclesiastical Sonnets,* or a vacation climbing in the Vale of Chamonix using its thin air and frigid glaciers to lift your soul into the Sublime, "the mighty vision passing there/As in her natural form," away from the sullen spectacle of science turning into your fifth-grade grammar teacher to diagram the bronze syntax of a sentence of Nature burnished a pale beer color from all the hands that have glided through it trying to grasp it like the rung of a ladder let down in front of you to help you climb the marble wall of history or life or experience as if that didn't also mean Jackie grabbed Lillian's crotch.

4.
But if I go that way and allow a denim-shrouded body to consume as much memory as the painting by the minor Baroque artist we saw at the Boston College art museum of the Penitent Magdalen of legend who was lost at sea and foundered on the south of France to minister with healing unguents made from the earth that drank of the blood of Christ spilled at the foot of the cross: Magdalen, young against all truth, resting on her side beneath a tree, reading a book, *momento mori* skull at her feet, her buttery breasts exposed: Lillian in a gravel-topped parking lot, talking and standing with her weight on one leg, the other leg

casually drawn over it to accentuate her V, all the codes and information packets that rain through the ionosphere all the time crushing into your brain unless you wear a skullcap made of Reynolds aluminum foil, then we choose to inhabit the space to the side where things live by themselves.

Naming Race Horses

1.
This is not a good day for naming race horses.
Everything is what it is and not what else it is.
One mailman coming up to the apartment building,
and maybe now's the time for a little offshore wading
with a car fender around my neck.
Fifty mailmen, perhaps with old style leather mail,
each a letter from you,
would be different. It sure was different, he said
back from Japan.
Going To The Orient is a good name for a horse.
I have never been to the Orient,
I have never been on a reconstruction of a Viking sailing
   ship.
Reconstruction Of A Viking Sailing Ship
is not a good name for a horse.

2.
Walking down to the East River
we saw a wood shack on a sandy
riverbank under the Manhattan
Bridge. I didn't think you
could find a riverbank anywhere
in the city, a real one, not
landfill like what used to be
the "Art Beach" near the Battery.
The shack had sky-blue
plastic sheeting for a roof
and a kind of porch or entryway
open to the river, which, as I
think of it now, was calm.
It looked like a nice place to live,
all things being equal: a view
of the river and its traffic:

garbage scows, tankers from around
the world, beautiful wood on cabin
cruisers from the thirties,
a golden age of yachting. Plenty
of rats too, I bet. We climbed
down to look at it: no one "was
home" but since it was the city
we didn't get too close to make
sure: we were sort of in awe
of the place, its integrity,
I can't find a better word.
I thought, I want to live here:
I could have the city, shore,
a river at my feet,
the accumulating bubble of history
to breathe in but not be
reflected on to, a sense of time
giving volume to things like Grimm's
Law, the *t*'s turning into *d*'s.

3.
I thought it was getting dark but, no,
a light rain has been falling,
the street is just wet
except for a tan-ish patch where a car
was parked, the usual invisible
layer of dirt you'd expect
under a car

is not a good name for a horse.

4.
And you broke the rhyme I could use
to forget about it.
I broke it first — true,
but what remained had a certain logic
if by "logic" I mean you could

understand it after twenty years,
twenty million dollars, a life spent
camping out on ridges along cell linings,
following migratory herds, learning
rules for elision of vowels in
certain forms of address. Your leaving
was expected and still it was news —
the fireworks company blowing up —
news because it was expected and could
be recognized when it was, the scale
for such things completely lost,
forgotten, what does it matter.
We never took a walk on the West
Side Highway, now it's being torn down,
has been torn down, never stole
one of the highway medallions
with the Indian and the Pilgrim.
When did we go to the New
Music store, if ever?
I never returned a meal.

5.
And what name can I give
to see things develop like children,
visit with sometimes, ask how
they're doing as I have become —
it doesn't matter how detailed
or true because someone is always
drawing maps of the real world:
in one Triton blows his horn,
another follows the PATH train to
New Jersey, first through a layer
of rock that was good for digging in,
then aboveground through wetlands that
flush the North River, a name
tugboat people use for the Hudson
when it becomes less what you would

paint if you were part of the
Hudson River School and upper-New
York State removed layers of dream
and history you had better love,
says the city, or you will die
useless in the background which
doesn't exist either, just
try and find it. It's going
right through you, says a cricket
in the house and makes you think
of a lot of things, but basically
wants out with the other crickets.
Boring green all summer, now these
bell-shaped flowers coming out of
nowhere, or not out of nowhere
since I've seen this before:
I like the Michaelmas daisy and
the smoky blue flowers on the other
side. I like the days getting shorter
(I liked them getting longer, too):
I like shopping for something to
make dinner with at 6 o'clock in
the evening when people are getting
home and it's already dark.
I like buying bread and bright yellow lemons.
I like to buy the wine or the beer,
I like to say "I'll fix drinks"
and I like cutting a peel of lemon.
I like WNEW-AM with Julius LaRosa.
It won't matter how detailed or true
because it is impossible.
It won't matter because my
wishes were constant the first time
I saw any of this, so exactly it fit
the way I knew I wanted to have it.

Pilgrims Undaunted by Speed

at the dedication of the Aeronautical Environmental Research Lab, MIT

Two days before the annular eclipse in Boston, I went to the North End and had a cannoli from Mike's Pastry. This has nothing to do with the eclipse, but it tasted so good I thought I should say something about it: Mike's Pastry has the best cannolis in the North End. No one has ever said this in a poem, and for a poet, as for a research engineer, it is important to a) get it right and b) do it first. When I was a student, I used to go to the North End every Friday for dinner at Felicia's Restaurant with Jennie (love is flight), and for dessert we'd get spumoni and ask for claret sauce, which at that time they served in a decanter, letting you pour the claret sauce over the spumoni, thick as you pleased. Today, during the eclipse, I stopped grading final reports (which by the way were very good — language is flight, too), and went outside to watch everybody watching the eclipse. I saw the moon darken the sun through a pin-hole in a piece of cardboard, then moved to a clump of people looking at it do that in a box. The best was a student who set out a bowl of water and through what I think were photographic plates looked at the eclipse reflected off the surface of the liquid. He let me do it ("How did you think of that," I asked: "I go to MIT!" he said in perfect explanation), and when I looked through the photographic plates, the crescent sun's reflection looked red as claret sauce. I go to MIT too, in a way, so I curled my index finger down into the space between it and my thumb to make a perfectly round pin-hole and modeled my version of the eclipse on the sidewalk in front of me, held literally in the palm of my hand the mystery of darkness in its flight across our day.

Summer Baby

I was nineteen, swimming
off Rockaway and was caught
in an undertow stronger than usual
because of a hurricane out
in the Atlantic. The storm was very
far away, not anything imminent (I
don't take chances like that) and
I was scared not panicked
as the current pulled me
straight out from shore.
I figured the thing to do was not
to try swimming in directly — it
was too strong, I could feel
it around my waist — but if I
swam at an angle I might over
distance catch the shoreline
curving out down the beach,
past one, then two,
finally three jetties
that broke the beachfront
at regular intervals.
                    I was nineteen
and knew this counted as the real thing.
I could have — not been swept out to sea —
but, worse, had to call for help
(I almost did) and was young
enough to feel embarrassed at being
the focus of all the strangers who'd
think (I thought) I was a poor swimmer
and drowning because of that, not
because of a storm way offshore
sucking water into its mouth like
one of the four winds in an old map.

At the beach everyone is looking for
something else to focus on
and I didn't want to be it.
I struggled, I won and got back safely,
kind of expecting cheers from
everyone I now hoped was watching.
I walked back to my towel feeling
pretty good about the way I'd handled
it, not panicking which is the worst
thing to do. I sat down
breathing a little harder,
a little more scared, thinking
about my tan, about turning
twenty, how strange
it is being a summer baby.

At the end of that same season
I was leaving the beach, heading for
the Green Line Bus (this was
a private bus service —
the buses were older
than city ones and had
rounded fronts that must have
been thought of as aerodynamic,
modern. The crowds on this line
were nicer — crammed in as
usual, but we were all
going to the beach on the beach bus
so we felt special)
and I walked right into
a flock, a drove, a lot of monarch
butterflies all heading one way.
This was right after *National Geographic*
had published photographs of a mountain
in Mexico where all of them go: strange
and slightly disturbing pictures

to see them covering everything: I
wanted to scoop them up with an ice-
cream scoop. I had stumbled into a part
of that secret (the magazine made a
point of not disclosing where it was)
between the hedges and metal railings
that snaked people on to a bus in Queens.
It might have been September, but late
August sounds right: summer for me
has always felt over by late August:
some leaves, of sycamores especially,
have already turned a dead papery
brown and lie, just a few, flat out
on the grass: pollution maybe, but
it's enough to see what's coming
and to begin wanting it now that
summer — nineteen, remember — has
shown you who you fell for.
I must not have fallen for anyone
and vice versa if I was alone,
but it didn't matter too much —
there was time and autumn up ahead
wearing a new sweater. I knew
what was going to happen
as I knew (didn't anyone
wonder about a kid that
far out?) I could make shore.

A Vision of Ted Berrigan in Cambridge, Massachusetts

I woke up late today and saw Ted Berrigan's stomach across the sun. Jennie! I cried, my hand over her side —

"She can't hear you," said Ted, "I doped her up" ("the girls!" I thought), "Them too, but it's harmless stuff and I want you to deliver a message," as he handed me a cigarette and a can of Pepsi. I don't smoke, I said. "Well, maybe you should — it hasn't been that long since I was in, not your, but my shoes, and aren't you a bit too concerned about health, living long, as if it were a possession?" Dangerous times, I said. "So, you think you can, metaphorically speaking, crawl inside and hide there? For what? Later?" Easy for you to say, you're dead, but

I'm honored, I said (trying to change the subject), soon my volume of poetry . . . "Save it," he said, "I'm not here to talk about that, I want you to take a message to somebody — oh don't sulk, maybe someday someone will visit and talk about your work, which is, you know, a crummy expression — your work, as if you weren't a ladder falling through the air, rungs all color and cognizance." You worked all the time, I said. "Oh, the sorcerer's apprentice gets a little feisty," he said, and threw a sucker-punch, which I easily deflected: "Nice," he said, "watch this," and went into a kung-fu crouch, frozen, "I have a message for you," I heard from behind me and turned around to see him sitting at a brown desk in a blue shirt. "It's a trick you learn, and they were very upset when I wrote about it in *The Sonnets*, which was too close for comfort." They? *"They shmey:* I have a message for you:

"Tell him he is more generous than Johnny Appleseed: here, have a tree is what it's like when you talk with him.

Various, orphaned, lost, you turn and wave your hand over the head of a friend who is dying while the oriental girl walks softly around the melting snow, a bunch of flowers in her arm, reaching for her keys with her other hand, thinking about what she has to do before her dinner party on the top floor of the apartment building where she lives. The light is getting longer each day and she greets her guests with a hug, presses her cheek to the side of the head. There is nothing he can do about it: his friend is not taking his leave, imperious in that it can't be any greater than this image of loss, and everything will have to catch up with that. Be careful: dreams are backed with industrial-strength canvas, tarred-over against the weather: they're very tough, they beat you up . . . ,"

and he reached out with his hand as if to touch me on the forehead, which I deflected to avoid the smudge I knew it would leave, the spot I saw beneath his eye. I did kung-fu. Meanwhile, my image collected the girls and ran downstairs where it met me outside. I looked up at the apartment window and saw Ted's form gently brushing the hair from Jennie's sleeping face. That was close, she said beside me, her dark, her oriental hair that I knew one day would save me.

All the While Knowing

The bet we made was whether
those wood tanks on buildings
downtown were used to collect
rainwater. They sit
on top of luxury condos
like African huts and I
couldn't imagine the Health
Department would let anyone
drink out of them given the
bacteria count their disease meters
would probably register.
You said the tanks maintained
water pressure, which sounded
official (you work for the city)
and technical. I think you won
the bet which was the kind
friends make with friends
when they would like to do more
for them even if it already
seems enough. All the right times,
exhilarated and adept, that don't
add up or subtract. I suspect
a natural law of some kind is
at work here, like the one that
dumps heavy snowfalls on the
Plains states while the Northeast

enjoys record mild temperatures.
In both places the homeless
freeze to death one by one,
part of a larger constellation
of other deaths. Percentages
are duly recorded only to

stare back at you like an
odalisque in a secondary work
of the last century, or like
the illustration I saw when I
opened the dictionary to check
the pronunciation of the word
odalisque: our lives remain
something that is permanently
their own like the Oregon Trail,
dotted here and there with settlements
and forts, an entry on the same page
with all those other entries, like
organdy, origin.

How People Swim

"It pays to be good at it,
climbing with one hand free,"
how some people swim on their side
like picking apples.

Not as if the word voyage was wrong.
It gets built in
walking around all day clapped in straw.

And it is a voyage of sorts.
Sometimes there is this pleasant feeling,
like having alphabetized a big stack of papers,
the shock of recognition as your name fits in
among asters and loosely falling
snow. Did you think it wouldn't? This is

the right season for this time of year.
I go to the laundromat late one night
and mosquitoes are all over the place,
so I stand outside by the door and read a book.
A linden tree is coming into flower at the curb.
There's this car parked near it, and I lean up against
the nice, shiny round part above the front wheel,
the quarter panel, just made for leaning on (or
for a kid, sitting on — at what age do we stop sitting
on cars?) and watch some people walk by.
I can't go anywhere because I have to be inside
when the door locks automatically at eleven.
I brought the right book to read, easy to put down,
eager to pick it up again. People stroll by (and that
is the right word, "stroll: to walk leisurely
as inclination directs"), and I'm perfectly aware
of how good all this feels without stretching it.

Without thinking about it, I was riding the crest
of this distraction I was putting off, and there was
a sense of depth and light in it, of not being able
to touch bottom, the surface billowing up as it
does sometimes when you least expect it to,
and it's still the surface but what else is it?
The Pakistani who speaks very little English
stared at me trying to stuff two sleeping bags
into the machine and nodded "yes" when the lumpy
side I pushed down made the other side pop up:
Encouragement? That's the way things are?
This is funny, do it again? It gave us something
to talk about while we were waiting to be bored
if by talking I mean nodding and making
our hands push down on the air and laughing.
I didn't enjoy the feel of lifting soaking wet
sleeping bags out of the wash — heavy as a drowned
man — but they were light as birds from the dryer
whose giant drum makes everything new.
Now if I use the word that means it was not oblique,
it doesn't match the streams of jet exhaust
and the sun going down behind the grassy dunes.
That was when I was happiest this time,
that was completely new. Didn't you know it?
Completely silver from the action of the waves,
a tree branch big enough to be the trunk, smooth
and already sand banked up behind it, becoming
part of the shore after it was part of the sea.

The Mummy

Here is a poem I wrote the other day: How many times have we heard that at a reading? And what are we supposed to be impressed with: the natural, unrehearsed genius of the poet who is all mouth and lightning? Is it an appeal not to take it seriously, or that the poet isn't taking it too seriously and just wants to please us (which isn't entirely a bad thing)? I mean, who would say here is a poem I wrote twenty five years ago and have been working on every day since — so tight is the construction of this poem you'd need an enema syringe the size of Fort Ticonderoga to loosen it up. Ethereal. Or is it a belief in the connection between poetry and life, which makes sense in that poetry isn't a criticism of life, or criticism isn't poetry, and that if life (I won't even begin to define the term) isn't poetry, what is it? While I'm not defining terms I also won't define poetry since what I recognize as poetry you may not and what's the point of making a big deal about it? Or if poetry is life (since terms at either end of an equals sign are identical) then maybe I should make a big deal about it, the way life does: remember how you used to get beat up in grammar school if you weren't careful, and even if you were? The time we hiked across Prospect Park to the Brooklyn Museum to see the Indian child mummy and on the way back these kids jumped us, and how I was able to keep this jerk away from me by swinging my toy army rifle around me like a helicopter blade? My friend was wearing an army helmet and I don't remember being asked to check our rifles and helmets at the museum. I guess you just know if someone is playing seriously and you go along with it, our mission that day to see what a dead child looked like.

Boston Italy

for Ben E. Watkins

Or because I used to see this girl every time I went for a run lying on her side reading a book in these jeans I couldn't help staring at, which is impolite, but it was like I wanted to be a painter, not actually go over and talk to her, which would look weird, a guy stopping in the middle of a run to go over and talk. I know someone who is a photographer and who does nudes and she said that's just what you do, "I go over and say 'I am a photographer and I would like to photograph you in the nude'" and no one goes shrieking out of their minds to the police, some say no thank you, others get an appointment and show up at her studio and she doesn't jump on them, she is a professional like a doctor and can think straight. Painters and photographers have it made because they need models like that. I can't say "I am a poet, and I would like to write about you in the nude," meaning her in the nude. I don't need a model. But I think, even though I can't touch-type, looking up at her lying there naked and then back down at these keys would be something I would like to try out.

Cigarette, Giotto, Tough Guy

Kerry Set for Joe Brainard

French Blue Jacket

French blue jacket
French blue morning

— WILLIAM CORBETT, untitled poem

Equally the fair and good
in the world touched lightly
by some balm,
an imprint of loss like a new coin
or median point that won't desert you.

Light goes through and through the night
shaping up like bleachers in a dry field
or hamadryads in confusion,
like two pages facing each other in a book.

Light,
which so many of us have given thanks for,
severs the arms of ancient statues
and covers the fields with healing compounds.
It shines brightly on mixtures of white cement
and assists nautical students in their work.

All this it does essentially undirtied.

Matters of greater importance
may be reserved for periods of longer duration.
A rectangle whose proportions
were three to five
was thought by the ancients
to be more beautiful than a perfect square.
History is everything a diagram
excludes on the surface of a plane.

But if we imagine
lifting it out of this plane
so that its sides drop downward
like an aerial cliff,
how differently we would view it "in time,"
standing at its edge and looking out,
looking at the sea, at the drowning grid,
hearing the only syllables we can memorize
as now you must.

Lycidas Algorithm

and such and such were coming before my eyes
— EIBHLÍS NÍ SHÚILLEABHÁIN
Letters from the Great Blasket,
December 12, 1951

1.
ach / mo / lena / marbh

After the things you have to do that nothing I say would be like this, or argue a wave of clarity and compulsion out of the night terms I, I, I: instead of a case, a word, a name.

but / my / with her / the dead's

2.
galar / mo / múineadh

So it proved true. And it was natural then that you would take it past the courthouse, then the cottage with livestock on the roof, then the fields that went on and on until you really walked them and saw that they only began like a throaty song cursing your enemies, or whole numbers that added up quickly and easily without fractions or decimal points dangling their jewelry from your neck and ears. Dreams like bees in work boots humped the field before you so that everything was in terms you knew by heart.

sickness / my / teaching

3.
bháite / heagla / ar / Téanam / leat / seasamh

A parallel would be useful here. Funny how things turn out, isn't it? I'm going away for a little while. I'll miss you too, but I need some time by myself. There, that's better. What happened while I was away? There was a lot of disease and conditions were poor. You'd want to draw a line made out of water, your back pulling against the surface, all the things you are saying to yourself.

drowned / fear / she said / Come / with you / standing

4.
ea / gliondar / ndeilbh / mar / anois / agam

You will have to say God is your father. You will have to say they have gone before you. Meanwhile the septic tank gurgles its consciousness of a job well done. The telephone rings off the hook of language and thought sticking in your throat, and jumps back into its hooded waters, adrift on the current. The matchbox family celebrates another birth. There is a blur who goes before you. You will have to say he is your father.

then / gladness / shapes / like / now / at me

5.
breá / bhfuil / agus / Buachaill / agus / Bhlascaod Mhór / thiar

Your eyes get used to the Atlantic curtain of the way we go without the mouth of leaves in salt air, Jimmy: Jimmy my friend, who are what I know about the things that are before me and after me and along with me, and what I'd want know anyway Jimmy, they are like you, amaryllis.

fine / is / and / The boy / and / the Great Blasket / in the west

(Words in Irish selected by chance from *Fiche Blian Ag Fás*, published in English as *Twenty Years A-Growing*, by Muiris Ó Súilleabháin.)

The Living End

Who are we to forget so much?
> — WILLIAM CORBETT

I remember
> — JOE BRAINARD

I forget the name of my fifth-grade true love who Danny Abel with the harelip also liked.

I forget the last four digits of the telephone number we had when I was growing up on 261-14th Street in Brooklyn which began HYacinth 9-. I thought it was the best telephone number in the whole world.

I forget when the phone company switched from names of things to numbers for telephone exchanges.

I forget the name of the assistant principal of Bishop Ford High School. One day he took over Brother Francis's religion class to give us sex education. He said he'd answer any question we wrote down anonymously on index cards. We wrote the dirtiest things we could imagine just to hear him read them out loud because his face, which was always a cartoon-color red, turned purple when he was agitated. To the question "What is a blow job?" he answered "When you put your penis in someone's mouth — and who would want to do such a disgusting thing?" Brother Timothy was the principal, and it bothered me that he had such a "weak" sounding name.

I forget the name of the boy who sat in front of me in Brother Francis's religion class. He played bassoon in the school band and was very shy and one day he was sitting at his desk just staring down at his religion book when the boy who sat in front of him was acting up. Brother Francis walked over to our aisle to smack the kid who was misbehaving, but he hit the bassoon player by mistake. This shy boy must have been hurt, but he was so surprised by this attack that he just stared up, open-mouthed, at Brother Francis who said "I'm sorry" and then — and this really cracked us up — never hit the kid who was causing the trouble. Brother Francis had a deep, low voice and his head was as big and bald as Elmer Fudd's and we called him Taras Bulba, not after the movie but because his head looked like a light bulb.

I forget the name of the rock band I managed in high school because I couldn't play an instrument or even sing, but I wanted to be part of the scene. Freddie Argenziano on drums, Joe and Charlie Legato on rhythm and base guitar, Steve Carlozzi lead guitar, John Colantoni voice, Bob Palmieri electric keyboard. We played at a happening directed by our drama teacher who later died of AIDS.

I forget when "happenings" stopped.

I forget, now and then, that Theresa is my mother's middle name until I see her sign a check *Beatrice Theresa Barrett*. Her doctor's office receptionist is a black woman from Jamaica who pronounces my mother's first name "Ba-treece," and I like to think of my mother being rechristened at the end of her life with a new name and a new ethnicity.

I forget if I ever thought I wouldn't die. I think I did think that, but I was afraid that everyone else would and I'd be left all alone.

I forget — and this would be sometime later — when I realized the world is just the way I would have wanted it to be, except for the really bad things that can happen, but

I'm lucky in my friends and look how beautiful some people are.

I forget the name of one of my swim coaches in grammar school who always showed up late to practice on Thursday evenings at John Jay High School where once a young black girl stood on a third-story ledge and threatened to kill herself and the crowd below chanted *Jump jump,* which made it into *The Daily News* the next day. My nickname on the swim team was Splash. The other coach, Eddie Smith, had a scar from a knife attack from his ear to his mouth. He went to St. Augustine's which had the coolest purple school jacket.

When I was five, I forget what I said to convince Janie Farrell to step over me as I lay on the ground in the courtyard behind our apartment building so I could look up her dress. I think I just asked her to do it and she thought it was a good idea too.

I really am surprised that I can't think of many more names of the kids I went to Holy Family Grammar School with. Danny Abel, Doreen Gogarty, Michael Matthews, Joeseph Cusamano, Lewis Livesey. Elaine who shared a desk with me and peed her uniform in the afternoon. The name of the boy who had a nose bleed when we stood up for afternoon prayers and a huge booger was dangling from one nostril so he turned around to share this with all of us in his row, hopping from one foot to the other until Sister Kevin Therese slapped him on the side of his head and the booger went flying into the next row of children. We wanted to laugh, but she smacked him really hard so we stood even more rigidly and recited the next *Hail Mary*.

I forget the words to the lullaby my father made up which began *ritchie ritchie roona*. . . .

I forget when Patrick Barrett, who came over from Ireland, erected the family headstone in Holy Cross Cemetery. 1838 or 1878. Over dinner recently at a Korean restaurant my mother suddenly announced that she wanted to be cremated. Bibimbop, chicken teriyaki, fish stew and extra kimchee all around.

I have two middle names (Charles William) and I forget who the Charles is I was named after.

I forget what the comic said when five of us went to the Country Club on 7th Avenue in Brooklyn the night we graduated from high school. We wore tuxedo jackets and I had my National Honor Society medal draped around my neck. Our chapter was named after the medieval scholar Duns Scotus, which we changed to Dumb Scrotum. The comic saw us walk in all dressed up and I think he said "Here come the virgin pimps." His act was mainly insults, and every now and then he'd whip "it" out, made of rubber a foot long and connected to a container of water in his pants which he sprayed over the audience and we all shrank back because even though we knew better it still felt like pee. I forget how long we stayed, but we left feeling like we had enjoyed the show which was packed even though it was an ordinary Wednesday night. Two of us went on to college, two went into the Marines and one was thrown out for being gay. I forget who the fifth boy was. I can't even picture him sitting at our table, laughing with the rest of us.

Flame Coat

1.
It takes this boy to throw so hard if you could save yourself, a flame coat to put a watch over a field or, to make itself laugh in a way we don't know, a catch in his voice as the river remembered it—in our years—later: not *for* him but *completely:* pre-canceled cells in his body turning in their homework over the Internet. The search was for the leaf-covered spot that could not be wounded, where no blood showed, ever, on the troll cot.

2.
Heard stars are sweeter, a couple of ideas all swirled up like a cowlick you can't brush down, distanced in the thought of stopping: the grass all nice and sticky, a barn that looks like it could never be mistaken in anything you do with it, accommodating its timbers to change as sturdily as fate with bits of straw in your hair.

3.
The ordinary phone patch, played into the milkweed, turning your name over in my mouth. The river pushes him down *for later* when it'd be sister or brother to something to be: postmark on a stamp filming the day, catch in the voice as you might say *forever and ever*.

4.
Mottled like a turtle's shell, cracked shearling, everything at its own cause the way it wanted to be, not without specialness but not special either, or alone: brother with brother, brother with brother and sister, sister with sister, all the way up and down the line, a team much stronger than yours, and no letting go of the moonlit axle.

5.
Attributes and qualities rustled through it, mind-reading without tongues or ripeness, not even what road the ground takes. Flame coat on the Gran Torino remembered him, put sweetness in his voice to catch him thinking about it for the river who had pushed him down that he could throw so hard, the drive-in screen like a postage stamp on the night sky.

6.
And all this for-ness, how they stood ten to the timber in peaked hats. And if you could save yourself to throw so hard, the river pushes him down to remember this of him — for him, something of it, that he could change back.

Intimations of Immortality

for Charles North

For Best Sandwich: BLT, Grilled Cheese, Ham and Swiss On Rye

For Best "Joy Of . . .": Joy of Cooking, Joy of Sex

For Best Word When You See It In A Poem By Wordsworth You Know He'd Have A Cow If He Knew How We Used It Today: gay, queer

For Best Food Additive: BHT, Nitrites, MSG, Red Dye #5, Red Dye #7

For Best Thing I Was Ever Told In The Morning: "You Were Laughing So Hard In Your Sleep You Woke Me Up," "No School Today, Ed, There's A Snowstorm," "Breakfast's Ready!"

For Best New Name For A Sexual Practice Among Consenting Adults: "The Cyclops Wears a Halo," "I'm Putting Out The Cat, Dear," "Fidel Castro"

For Best You Figure Out A Category: George Sanders' Brother In *The Seventh Victim* And *Cat People* (1942), Patrick Swayze's Brother I Once Saw On A Late Night Rerun Of *Geraldo*, Sylvester Stallone's Brother Who Wrote The Music For Some Of The Rocky Movies

For Best Literary Award: The Pulitzer, A MacArthur, The Nobel

For Best Way To Die: Easefully, Heroically, Screaming Out All The Saints' Names In Heaven Because You Never Really Believed It Would Happen To You, Unknown

For Best Horror/Sci-fi Memory (Late 50's, Non-Sickening): Attack Of The Fifty-Foot Woman (Her Buckskin Skirt), Attack Of The Fifty-Foot Man (His Scarred Face)

For Best Philosopher (Greek or Roman): Aristotle, Plato, Lucretius, Epictetus, Jesus

For Best Thing I Want To Know More About: The Liza Minnelli-Martin Scorcese Marriage, Life After Death, Life On Other Planets

For The Only Joke I Can Remember Right Now: What Do You Get When You Cross A Penis With A Potato?

For Best Moment In The Iliad: When His Horse Tells Achilles He (Achilles) Doesn't Have Long To Live, Death Of Patroclus, When Helen Appears On The Tower And The Old Men In Troy Understand What All The Fuss Is About, Hera Seduces Zeus Because She Knows He Always Falls Asleep After Sex And She'll Able To Slip Away And Make Life Hell For The Acheans, Hector Running From Achilles And Seeing The Places He Played In As A Kid, Achilles Dragging Hector's Body Around The Walls Of Troy, Priam Ransoming Son's Body, Funeral Games

For Best Thing I Can See In This Room Right Now: My New Answering Machine, A Mont Blanc Fountain Pen, Blue Jeans Faded Just Right, Blinds Blowing In From Breeze That Will Make It Easy To Sleep Tonight

For Best Title Of A Trilogy (Unmade): "Cigarette, Giotto, Tough Guy;" "Posse, Cupid, De-Calibrate;" "Valence, Cherry, Motorboat"

For Best Excuse: "You Know I Love You," "I Missed The Stupid Train," "I'll Never Do It Again"

And the winners:
BLT, *Joy of Cooking*, gay, MSG, "No School Today, Ed, There's A Snowstorm," "The Cyclops Wears A Halo," George Sanders' Brother In *The Seventh Victim* And *Cat People* (1942), A MacArthur, Heroically, *Attack Of The Fifty-Foot Woman* (Her Buckskin Skirt), Lucretius, Life After Death, What Do You Get When You Cross A Penis With A Potato?, Death Of Patroclus, Blinds Blowing In From Breeze That Will Make It Easy To Sleep Tonight, "Cigarette, Giotto, Tough Guy," "I'll Never Do It Again"

Seen in the audience were: Mr. and Mrs. Hot And Cold Running Water; Death, with the lovely young starlet, Life; actress Spring Mattress; 69 with European star Swiss Army Knife; actor Bic Pen; new singing sensation, Tongue; the adorable young child-star from the hit movie, *You Can Pick Out, Like, What, Five Constellations?*, Potato Chip; Without Rhyme; and Reason.

Archery

In that clear way

we go for a walk at night
and the dark takes in the last part
like a true dome, which refers
just as much to what it excludes.
In a forest you belong to
one tree then another.

The recent past was only
parallel. The unique event
shining in the silver cup
of the inner ear is preserved
by the semi-precious amber
of characteristic gesture
and account,

cutouts for the season in line
with the next one
like a school play.

But we enjoy the helpless parts.
The day is all around
like parachute silk and
Greek tragedy:
we go poking on ahead
or driving hard at the clear point,
nipple and twining cord
above the sword grass.
I have always wanted this light

and to become visible in a new way for you,
adequate or inadequate to consolation,

to the secret's in the surface part of things,
thumb and forefinger pressing lightly together
the trajectory in an open
scene for milk and the elements of milk.

Three Italian Sonnets for Mark Morris

I.
Everyone walks on
Place-names fall back on countries printed in orange
You are not that one: happy, happier
Or with little as curbing matters appear
Happy
               I am reaching you goodbye

Some of the changes are minor who walked among them
This is another room
constant pressure on another moment
sailing off now, listing
goodbye goodbye to a defter air
like children
Our pleasures are worth informing
There's honor there too

II.
And if you appear in a moment
some of the changes are minor,
everyone walks off:
There are moments in fall

little information and back to the room
walks in the country
constant pressure of minor changes
sails now listing, now falling back
the air deftly matting everything

The printing fell back on everyone who had not sailed off to another country but who now were happier. The room listed. A constant sum of appearances were forming their own: you reaching off the curb, the one, minor country as a place, as a moment falling or naming you. Children appeared like print, like walking each other among the oranges. Information was constantly being exchanged about country rooms, place-names, and deft minor pleasures. I am pleased to inform you that your name is now honored among those who walk in the air. Please print your name. Now another one. And in the fall they change.

III.
I am printing you on another one
This moment was there too
Deft and happy were the rooms when you walked among
   them in orange
Everyone changes,
changes are honor too, our worth
is pleasure, airy
and always sailing off with another name
Who was ever minor when they were happy?
I placed the names of some countries on the curb,
what matters is that you were listing some of them too

And in the fall they change
some are orange and sail off
I walk among the countries at my back and you appear
Everything is another child, a way back, loyal

Night for Day

after looking at a page in Vietnamese

I go to church. This is the Year of Steeples.
This is The Rung To Try The Minds
and repeat. But to show me the way
is the Irish of Strong Bow,

the you of the impersonal and the land of ruong ma,
which means bat and Ma'm and très bien,
giddy you of the impersonal
like song in the vocal mind,

song dem gonna sang
can I, can you of the impersonal
dem chop thee sang
three-rung you, ray-hipped,

dem lay thee down by the
cake, by the "tu" X-
Vang Man, now engage,
engage you name, impersonal.

Now can "you" engage "me"
behind the earlier appearing letters,
now of the day impersonal
now dem and you again

Can they sang as a form of
saw in the unlettered church of the
way trong,
you, always you, can going, me at,

you at Irish for house, my you of the Strong Bow,
X-Vang Man, what you, unmoving,
defaced beneath the letters,
continue

Lyrical Ballads

Lyrical Ballads

Vicki said she had a child from a previous relationship, and the ocean is the Saltines of time, to find not just yourself, the single grammatical soul fluttering like a syringe above the miniature Japanese forests of scrub oak on Nantucket, certainly not clarity or truth in the cross hairs of heaven. The ocean tosses its lace panties at your feet, and we'd like to have a voice in it, our lost soul, working part-time at Congdon's pharmacy after the divorce. The previous child absorbs changes of light on the ocean, maybe *is* the changes of light on the ocean, releasing them like cake for our pharmaceuticals during the intervals between sea captains returning with their stupid chanteys, receiving their traditional welcome: "Pee-yoo, is that whale piss I smell? Look out, I'm going to vomit!" Each of us is previous, a syntax of light and cake. Vicki said she'd like to be in a relationship again, the Japanese art of miniaturization applied to a nice new pair of panties shining white against her tanned legs. And though the soul as we know it is lost, except as a tasty Saltine like a mouthful of miniature ocean, out of its blubbery absence there is this love.

Antigone in Flatbush

Light takes these things apart,
even though this is our only way of seeing—
in parts—how some things are brilliant
on the surface and very white which the sun
illuminates so that they seem to dissolve
in a spray of light which they give off
like a fountain.
I like to think of the entire surface
lifting up like a mist with the light
as if we still didn't know the idea
of yesterday was impossible although we drag
it along for a while like it was the place
we are supposed to start from—a cave
that we think we keep crawling out of
when in fact the light is always just there,
a whiteness we are floating in.
Anyway, we expel yesterday as naturally
as our breath. The only part I would change
about history is the idea it really happened to us.
It never does except later on:
we keep opening up the same chapter,
the one about the empire failing, and how
the city doesn't seem as close to the shore
as we thought it must have been, otherwise
why did we cut down all those trees?
We tend to wash up just ahead of the recent past,
and still we hear these wonderful
innocent sounds in our ear, another morning. The whole
idea of just beginning at the point of
leaving off is hard to take. We want connections
but we also want it entirely new—
especially at the juncture of yesterday and today—
tomorrow is very advanced and already seems

crammed with things to do — so we step back
from it and find ourselves looking around
at all the equipment we have been left with
from before; today seems so abandoned,
and we are just the few survivors
of last night's catastrophe, the one
we didn't notice. But it must have happened.
Things have returned to themselves.

By noon the city is swimming in itself.
Even though it is contained by geography,
the charity of real time and real place
permits an infinitely complex, infinitely
divisible series of things to happen at once;
and if anyone tried to reconstruct how history
was made, they'd have a simple choice: either
witness every action everywhere, or admit your
defeat and think up comical themes and fundamental
stories explaining how and why you and I aren't
really you and I but the end result of forces,
just or unjust, beyond us.
Which of course we are because there is nothing
without pain, nothing grievous or without
delusion and shame that fate hasn't brought about.
But in between the rest of time
the real moment of true history is curling
its perfectly formed infant's hand around
another part of it all, which'd break off
if we tried to grab on to it since
we're being pushed along so fast by the day,
rushing out like the tide. Our clothes
feel heavy. There is this really pleasant sensation
to being naked late in the day. And evening, the light
is stationary, the city falls back upon itself,
the face of everything is composed, and our eyes
really open for the first time.

There's a soundlessness surrounding each action.
We walk around, but really
there isn't that much to do — the idea of searching
out what we already know — but now we have it.
At least at this point
we know we haven't got it, but it matters
that we see it mirrored there,
unless you think we're brought into the light of day
the way divers in Crete bring up octopus:
they can only hold their breath for so long,
so they wrap the octopus around
their legs and arms — an octopus will hold
on to anything, like an infant —
and when the divers surface all studded with
living things, they unwrap themselves,
bite the octopus beneath its newborn eye
and beat it against the rocks to make it tender.

The charity part I understand: how we slide
between the real events in other people's lives.
The only obstacle is on some other island
and we have this clear night to walk out into,
as if we were going to float up on the face
of the ocean. Only we aren't going to be left alone
this time, and we have this new kind of feeling
about everything; the whole city is new,
an entirely different place with immense mistakes
shining out of the stars, although we like it
that way. It's better to have certain things already
decided upon. And if we challenge them,
the only part we might wind up asserting
is how parallel sets of circumstances...
well, we just might discover they were better all along.
What I mean is, fate is about as useful a word
as octopus, but it means something — it means
in a different city there are people who look

and act exactly like us, only they have slightly
different ways of appreciating what they do,
and invent useful little things to help them
in very unimportant ways: only it matters
to them that they do it like this: a different
and to them better way of tying straps, for instance.
Or it means exactly the opposite:
all these characteristics — how we
tie our straps, the plaiting of our hair, the ordering
of flowers — these are the things we notice.
The rest of it, the fateful part, is all shot
through with hyacinth and the songs of birds,
with fig tree and myrtle, the dirt kicked up
and falling on your eyelash, the eyelash itself
sweeping the eye clean so it can focus on
the forward part of things: and the rest of it,
the gulf between, the really deep blue charter that
exists to talk about, and how evenly it spreads
around — petals that curl out of it,
or sounds that have to start from somewhere.
What's beautiful I suppose is that we hear it once —
it doesn't get caught up with meaning that way —
I mean, beyond itself; and that doesn't have to
mean anything. Civilization doesn't have to care
that it was said although it may be the only thing
that is remembered for totally unrelated reasons.
And meanings come floating up around it at night.
We can have only one mother and one father,
but we can always have more children. We want
it that way, both how we stem
from someone and how others stem from us.
And those others can be various, complex,
differing from one another so we can love them
all the more. They're individuals and in that
they are alive for us — although the "for us"
is the part we are secret to,

looking back at us with special favor, now they
understand, here is the special meaning,
you are the one I know; I love you.
Except love renews itself, even without us.
In summer these big heavy rainstorms seem more
like a sign of fullness and brevity. I've noticed
how we flatter anything that is young as if the fact
of opening up our arms were sufficient.
The only ones we want are around us everywhere.
The miraculous part is that our summery souls
fit exactly what we overlook. But what are we
that on such and such a day we should come face
to face with this unalterable new position
of the world? What before had been the blondest
sheathing of light cracks open to reveal
the pale green error curled up and beginning
to unfold its fiddlehead on the forest floor,
a forest that somehow shot up around it overnight,
and we accept it without too much questioning:
all that we mean by our own small and encompassing
life, the only uncharitable fact in the free
sprawl around us.

Two Poems for Kenward Elmslie

Snow

is falling past
the reserves of the
great nation
which in the late
nation are the snow,
detailing for us a part
of the nation
such as park or
bath towel.
And rising in the wind
like tinned-steel paper clips,
it crosses
over to the nation and
remains there.
It is the past.
And we who are in
the nation and around
the nation are concerned with it.
It is our powerhouse
it falls upon, and what if
it should collapse and grow silent?

For silence is the great
reserve of history,
filling our backs
with a snowy nation
although we jump into
and out of
the powerhouse in little spurts
like a glamor puss.
The scrunchy stuff
is gobbling up our feet

at the same time we go sliding
through it. And the nation,
threaded to itself beneath the snow,
hammers its history into a
silky power
which these little avowals
reserved for silence cross out.

Untitled

The course dealt with only a few major themes,
and we already have the questions, yet
the weekend before the final exam
is not much fun. We go out,
but we know the essay we started is waiting
like a half-eaten sandwich. The mimeographed
questions, a pale sky-blue, are vacant as
day under the darker netting of our scribbled
notes. We try to personalize the lessons
we thought we took away from each lecture,
but the facts lobbed over to us like magnesium
flares no longer illuminate an impressive
infantry of ideas wading ashore: they float
at our feet like dead fish we have to kick
away to go for a swim. We aren't classic:
we like a real test with right answers
when we step up to the examining table
and have our lute and fireman's hat
taken away. It should be serious,
not a matter of too much judgment
although the questions only scratch the surface
as we float backwards through them to the truth.

Secent Image

for Ann Lauterbach

1.

Even a faucet is greater, and the bright wrist asserts neither expectation nor ignorance, this incredible radiant traction we have. Won't you ever learn, each loss promoted on the branch of days, except now everything stands for everything else without recognition or fear or truth, plush and dark, filled with friends and stars clinking in your summer glass, music of confidence and despair? Or some mark you could lean against or cross with silage, knowing what is exacted, at least until description licks its finger and draws the outline of a boat on your lips. How will I be known? Nothing exceeds description which is bigger than necessity, a patchwork quilt that shows how we live in the dative case. One types *There are no silhouettes, canvas bass notes ascend the mirrored disc, not as cause or continuation, but how one winter I took off my gloves eager to chop ice out of a boat cover* and that this is all you ever wanted: to reclaim the parts of language and death that belong to you.

2.

But not for what they cannot offer to be known, a funny kind of absence of a refrain that nothing will ever be like this again. So many had been like description, a language of dying that is not about loss, *secent image* written with dignity, comprehension, error. A language of dying to implore this image: *Give me nothing back; this is for you; this is how I see you, I could trace you forever.* So they stand in for what is absent. You couldn't make them into anything else, and what they are is a set of tools for perception and leave-taking, something temporary for something permanent, which though not yet known is not *unknown* in terms we're now familiar with. So many had been like *description*. Not a photograph, at least not a photograph as you might hear it discussed on the T, at the Charles Street/Massachusetts General Hospital station, before the train arches its neck into the tunnel's black water again.

3.
Dr. Livingstein I presume? Memory isn't paginal: pointing to the mantle of falling leaves, it offers its critique of pure reason as being out of it, then rustles through the database as a portion of fate or recognition so that all entries smell faintly of tannin, braiding (or unbraiding) invisible cords of expectation and desire lashed to your wrist, shining like a kiss — not as knowledge or dimension, but that nothing can be greater than any image of our loss, and everything will have to catch up with that: knowledge *as only* description, a grammar of vanishing points like the slender dark cone of your voice so that the plane of surfaces doesn't just dissolve (we begin with that premise) or slant so fully in its descent that we walk between them, or disappear behind them or into them, reflected against these surfaces like graffiti, like leaves banked up against a wall.

4.
No, the reality of that never completes itself in us, a grammar that lets you see not what isn't there (we begin with that premise too) but *that it isn't there* is a recognition which includes, but is more than that which is now gone forever (although that never completes itself in us either). That's what memory is, isn't it? The other side of the photograph brought forward as the real subject, how we drift in a sort of sideways scallop motion through the page, piling up instances of these unknown conditions, or reflected by them in a kind of virtual presence. *That it isn't there* in the sense that each object describes what it just missed, so that it's funny how you see through them, yet delight in them because they are shed off like that.

5.
So the necessary conditions are unknown. On a wall someone writes *shadow* or *logic,* or *this arrogance will be your undoing mister demonicus* and sees right through it. Maybe not *to* anything, but that after all was where we started a minute ago. Memory then is just this sort of unspecific recognition that we're not going to see anything anyway, and that all we do is process (wordprocess if you like) descriptions of what we feel is missing. It's like you were disappearing sometimes. So these slant through the plane of the picture like a triangle, one leg declining over the other, completed by leaves banked up on the other side of the photograph. *Dear Angle.* One types *happiness and other forms of terror,* or *Loss, a new coin in your pocket* and *Don't be afraid, I went in there and I came out again,* heroic and kind, human too for what it cannot offer to be known in someone else's case, and ultimately how separated we are although in the early dark once the clocks have been turned back it's not the individual windows but the whole block lit up like an airplane turning out of the page of the sky, *Shudder in one leg of the journey.*

6.
Dear Angle, There are no silhouettes, falling out of the page of the sky, as if someone turned the photograph over to see what was written on the other side. This wall is made up of shadows and each one drifts sideways through the page of the day in a sort of scallop motion like a falling leaf, not as cause or continuation but how so many had been like description of some other object which they reflected or maybe sketched the outline of. But no, not what wasn't there, but there only after you saw it, *because* you saw it, which is important to remember, this portion of fate or recognition which you think is in there, how they drift down out of the day, and you feel you are looking *through* them to something else, not really *at* them. Never-

theless, they should be *pressed to your lips* as they used to say because they're not hiding anything, nor are they translations appropriating something that doesn't belong to them and, therefore, because they are dying, these things we have which seem to be about so many other things.

Song

for Michael and Isabel Pinto-Franco

Remember that day, Ed
   it was raining you
took the boat out
   bright yellow rainpants
and hood you
were the only child that had ever
      been born
The world was sliding past
   on rain and waves
broke over the bow
     the newly
varnished deck
   and beading rain
You
could have drowned and
   been a wave. Michael
and Isabel are having a
     baby
The world is just so un-
   protected we
can't stop loving it
   Ed, you know
you were not the
   only child,
your legs held down by
     waves
and hooded face
   of a boy